FOCUS, TRUST, & FOLLOW

FOCUS, TRUST, & FOLLOW

SHANA BYRD

Copyright © 2020 J Merrill Publishing, Inc.

All rights reserved. No part of this publication may be reproduced, distributed, or transmitted in any form or by any means, including photocopying, recording, or other electronic or mechanical methods, without the prior written permission of the publisher, except in the case of brief quotations embodied in critical reviews and certain other noncommercial uses permitted by copyright law. For permission requests, write to the publisher, addressed "Attention: Permissions Coordinator," at the address below.

ISBN: 978-1-950719-49-5 (Paperback)
ISBN: 978-1-950719-50-1 (eBook)

Library of Congress Control Number: 2020915457

Any references to historical events, real people, or real places are used fictitiously. Names, characters, and places are products of the author's imagination.

J Merrill Publishing, Inc.
434 Hillpine Drive
Columbus, OH 43207

www.JMerrillPublishingInc.com

I would like to dedicate this book to my inspiration, Tim, Quoran, Timmy Shane, Makhi, and Nasir.

CONTENTS

Introduction   ix

Part I
FOCUS
1. Check your rearview mirror   3
2. Escape Rooms and Waiting Rooms   5
3. He did it for me   7
4. Silently Loud or Loud in the Midst   9
5. Strength-Based   11
6. My Father's Approval   13

Part II
TRUST
7. Friends with better lives   17
8. From the Inside Out   21
9. God's Math   23
10. The Invisible Man Inside of Me   25
11. I Get It   27
12. Ground Hog Day   29

Part III
FOLLOW
13. GPS (God's Positioning System)   33
14. Oil Change   35

15. Open Book Test	37
16. Unrequited Love	39
17. Bankruptcy	41
18. Priceless	43
About the Author	45

INTRODUCTION

My book is a series of personal devotions that have been inspired by everyday life. I believe that God allowed me to see Him in everyday situations so that I can help make the Word plain for people to understand, including myself.

I was not raised in the church and gave my life to the Lord as an adult, so understanding Bible lingo was confusing and hard to relate to at times. I was able to take conversations with my children, along with other experiences, and turn them into "ah-ha" moments with God.

I hope that readers find my book relatable and applicable in their journey with Christ.

PART I
FOCUS

1
CHECK YOUR REARVIEW MIRROR
MATTHEW 25:35-40

My 16-year-old son is learning to drive and learning all the rules that come with that privilege. One thing that his instructor told him was always to check his rearview mirror and know what is behind him. The instructor found it to be such a valuable lesson that he even asked during the driving portion what color was the car behind my son. I thought that was an interesting point because I always check my mirrors. Still, I'm not sure that I have ever paid enough attention to what's behind me to the point that I noticed the color of the car behind me.

This lesson made me think about how we, as believers, can forget to check our rearview mirror. In fact, most of us have probably been taught to "keep our hand to the plow," and not to remember the past. However, a quick look in our rearview mirror can help us appreciate all that God has brought us through. So as I reflect on my life, I think of all the things God had healed me of, the moments when I was hungry but had no money to feed my family, and He supplied several meals for me. I even take a real quick moment to remember all the sinful things I have done, and He still loves me and is ever-present in my life. That glance in the rearview, for me, is just a moment for me to praise God and to appreciate how He is moving me forward in Him.

So in those moments where you may feel like you are in a spiritual traffic jam or stagnant in life, take a quick moment to check your rearview mirror and Praise God for what He has brought you through. Make sure it's a quick look because, as we have been taught, you cannot drive a car forward while staring in the rearview mirror because you will crash. The same is true of your life.

* I'm not at my destination but Praise the Lord that I have moved from my starting point. *

2
ESCAPE ROOMS AND WAITING ROOMS
LAMENTATIONS 3:19-26

I enjoy playing escape room games on my phone that require me to use different clues to escape a locked room. The game required attention to detail, memory, and other problem-solving skills to escape one locked room only to enter another. Each level is more difficult than the previous, and each level offers skills to prepare you for the next.

Playing these games and being locked in these rooms reminded me of being held up in God's waiting room. Even though God has a purpose for us in the waiting room, we still have the urge to escape. The objective of being in God's waiting room is to focus on God, trust Him through the wait, and follow His instructions. While we sit in

God's waiting room, He gives us the tools that we need that will eventually open the door and allow us to move forward in His purpose. The tools may not include clues with number codes on a clock or putting puzzles together. God uses whatever and whoever He wants. He often uses things like His Word, a conversation, and reminders of how God has brought you through. Then He presents the opportunity for you to minister to others. We, as believers, just have to be attentive to God.

The objective of being in God's waiting room isn't the "Great Escape." Instead, it is to focus on God and what He is teaching you in the moment. Just like the games I play on my phone, each lesson learned in God's waiting room is preparing us for a higher level.

3

HE DID IT FOR ME
JOHN 19:1-6 & 16-30

I don't know if it was the "Year of Survival," the outreach that our youth ministry had been participating in, or just life, in general, that had me "all in my feelings." Still, this Christmas, I woke up in awe of **my** Savior. As my mind raced over my life, my heart became overwhelmed, and my eyes swollen with tears. It is incomprehensible to think about how much Jesus loves me. The thought of all that He endured just to save me from the sins that I have chosen and at times still decide to commit is just surreal.

There will always be debates and controversy about Christmas, even among believers. Unfortunately, I believe that the true meaning of our celebration can be lost in the drama, politics, and even the commercialism. I think that whether Jesus was born on December 25th, the middle of the summer, or on some other random day of the year, is all irrelevant. What matters is that Jesus, the ONLY begotten son of God, was born for one reason, and that is to save us from our sins. So, to recap on how much He loves me, Jesus, the Son of God, chose me. My omnipotent God knew how messed up I was and all the messed-up things I would do in my future, and yet He was still born to die just for **me**.

Although traditionally we have reserved December 25th as the day to celebrate the birth of Jesus, we need to do it every day several times a day. Each day we should all take a moment just to reflect on our lives the good, the bad, the ugly, and all He has brought us through. Then imagine the hurt, pain, hatred, and how heinous His crucifixion that He endured JUST FOR YOU. Overwhelming!

4
SILENTLY LOUD OR LOUD IN THE MIDST
MATTHEW 6:1-8

Our second oldest son is usually the quiet one when we are outside of the home, especially in school. Ironically, his being so quiet in school became a problem with his teachers because they knew he had the answers, but he would not volunteer the answers. Normally, having a quiet child in school is not an issue. However, the fact that it bothered his teachers began to bother me. I wanted to push him to speak up more in school. God quickly reminded me not to pressure my son and just to trust Him in the situation.

One morning while getting ready for the workday, I peeked in on my son in his bedroom. He was kneeling on the side of his bed, praying.

Here he was, my 10-year-old son all alone in his prayer closet, spending time with his God. What the world has been seeing as a personality flaw, my God saw as an opportunity to spend time with one of His children. The more time my son spent alone with God in his prayer closet, the more he began to open up in school.

Matthew 6:1-8 instructs us to do good deeds and pray alone without an audience. It isn't about being in the spotlight and always getting recognition for all that we do. God is who we want to notice us. What we have done in secret, He will, in turn, reward us openly. (v.6). Each day we must get alone with God, forget about the hustle and bustle of the world, talk to God, and listen to what He has for us. Sometimes God speaks the loudest when we are the quietest.

5

STRENGTH-BASED

JOB 1:13-20; 42:7-16

*A*s an early childhood professional and parent coach, a lot of what we did was "strength-based." That meant we would set rules in the classrooms based on the desired behavior. For example, instead of the rule, No Hitting, it would say use gentle hands. We would also set goals for families and made sure the documentation was strength-based and focused on the positive. For example, instead of saying a parent was resistant to meeting with Child Protective Services, I would say that the parent has protective factors with a strong desire to keep her family intact.

This made me think, how often, as believers, do we share Jesus from a strength-based point of view? Whenever someone mentions Job, it's usually to emphasize all that he lost. We often fail to share how God gave Job back all he had lost and more. I'm guilty of focusing on the negative at times. I often forget to emphasize the fact that God brought me through whatever hardships I have experienced. I have to change my mindset and the language I use. I can't focus on the loss of a fantastic job, but on that, God opened the doors of new opportunities for me to move toward His destiny for me.

I challenge you to look at God from a strength-based point of view. What hard time has God brought you through? Try changing the language on that situation to it being a testimony so that God can get the glory He deserves.

6
MY FATHER'S APPROVAL
GALATIANS 1:10/MATTHEW 25:14-30

My dad and I were having a conversation one day. He recently had surgery due to cancer. This life-changing event sparked some very interesting topics between my father and me.

One of the topics that touched me the most was the one regarding my marriage. My dad told me how proud of us he was. He went on to say to me that he could not have picked a better husband for his baby girl. "Tim is a great guy, I love him," were my dad's exact words. Those words melted me. It was awesome to have my father's approval of the man that I have decided to spend the rest of my life with.

Soon after that time with my dad, I started to

think about how important his approval was to me. I began to wonder if I were that concerned about my heavenly Father's approval in all areas of my life. Every day God trusts us with different tasks, responsibilities, and tests to pass. How we handle what He has given us determines His approval of us. It is our honorable duty to take on every task with the mindset of wanting God's approval. At the end of each day, we long to hear our Lord say the words, "Well done, good and faithful servant." (Matthew 25:21). So as life happens and we are faced with decisions and situations, let us always be reminded of our everlasting desire to have our Father's approval.

PART II
TRUST

7
FRIENDS WITH BETTER LIVES
JEREMIAH 29:11

For years I beat myself up for the life I created for myself. It certainly was not the life I envisioned for myself. My ideal path was to finish college, become a pharmacist, get married, and have children. My reality is I was pregnant with my first child during the first semester of my freshman year of college. I dropped out, I got married by 21, had three more children by 26, and worked in several different companies as an early childhood educator. All this took place long before I got my bachelor's, which took 13 years to complete. My reality was nothing like my ideal life plan.

I often found myself comparing my situation to people who did things in the "right" order. I was ashamed and disappointed in myself and the hardships that I created. I looked at my friends that seemed to have it all together. They had better cars, houses, clothes, and more money. Simply put, they appeared to have better lives. Some of these friends even felt the same way about my life. They would offer advice on how to prioritize and manage my finances. I'm sure they had good intentions. Nonetheless, their intentions made me feel even more ashamed and discouraged. I felt this shame for years, which lead to depression, anxiety, and diminishing self-worth.

Amid this dark cycle, I heard God speak to me through Jeremiah 29:11. God assured me that the plans I made for myself were not the plans that He had for me. My way was not the "right" way, and the right way was His way. Even though it looked as if my friends had better lives, God showed me that my life was good. While they were busy building their physical houses, I was busy building my spiritual house and, ultimately, God's house. I was building the Lord's house by being a good wife and mother and providing a Christian foundation for my children to stand. By persevering through my trials, I have continued my path to becoming the woman God has designed me to be. Our ultimate goal as believers is not to have a picture-perfect life with all the superficial things that appeal to the flesh. Our ultimate goal is to glorify God. I have been able to give Him all the glory throughout the trials. They have strengthened my faith and offered me the opportunity to share my testimony or live my life as an example. So today, I am satisfied with the life that I live and recognize the value in all the things that I did not do my way but His way. It's God's way that has made me the wife, mother, and woman of God I am and keeps me anticipating what He has for me.

8
FROM THE INSIDE OUT
PSALM 51

My husband had a cyst on his leg that needed to be cut open. The doctor explained the wound would not be stitched closed because the infection needed to heal from the inside out. To someone in the medical field, they could see how well the healing process was going, but to my untrained eye, it just looked like an open wound until it was healed.

I'm reminded that this is precisely how our transformation in Christ works. When we accept Jesus as our Lord and Savior, our healing and cleansing begin. Initially, we may still look like a hurt and broken person on the outside. But, as we continue to walk with Jesus and live our lives accordingly, our outside appearance starts mimicking the work God has done on the inside.

Just like my husband's wound took time to heal and looked gross in the process. But once it was, the infection was gone, and the wound had been healed, no one could tell that it even existed. Invite Jesus into your life and allow the wound care to begin from the inside out.

9
GOD'S MATH
MATTHEW 6:25-34

I walked in on two of my sons having a discussion that didn't seem to be coming to an end anytime soon. Never-ending discussions between these two were very common. One is extremely logical in his thinking, and the other is more abstract, which made for some fascinating conversations. This discussion involved one son trying to prove that 2 and 2 are 5 instead of 4, as we have all been taught. I let my curiosity win and asked my son to explain his theory. His theory is as follows; 2&2 side by side is 22, V is the 22nd letter of the alphabet, and V is the Roman numeral 5, so therefore 2 and 2 are five. My son's theory is farfetched and had no mathematical truth to it but very creative and even well thought out.

I thought about my son's theory and how my other son could not wrap his mind around this theory because the numbers did not add up. It made me think about how we hesitate or refuse to take a step of faith because the numbers just do not add up or the way things are happening is not on our plan. It is so easy for us to talk our way out of what God is telling us to do because it just doesn't make sense to us. However, we must remember that we can't rationalize things of the Spirit. We have a particular outcome in our minds and the specific steps to get there, and when those steps are not being followed, we become afraid. But Ephesians 3:20 tells us that God is "able to do exceedingly abundantly above all that we ask or think, according to the power that works in us." How awesome is it that no matter how enormous our dreams are for ourselves, God has something bigger in store? To receive our "exceedingly, abundantly above," we have to trust God's irrational, illogical math and take the step of faith that He is calling us to take.

10

THE INVISIBLE MAN INSIDE OF ME

JOHN 14:26

One evening we were riding home from Bible study; the weather was rainy and windy. Stormy weather usually meant that my seven-year-old was a little nervous. He had always been afraid of storms, even to the point that we would warn his teachers of this fear. During this ride home, my son asked, "Mommy, what do I do if it storms tonight?" But before I could answer, he answered his own question. He said, "I know the invisible people inside of me will make me feel safe. They will read a story to me." I assure my son that indeed that there was one "person" living inside him, and it was the Holy Spirit.

The Bible describes the Holy Spirit as the Comforter. God sent the Holy Spirit to sustain us until the day Jesus returns. When we allow it, the Holy Spirit will lead us, speak through us, and comfort us in times of fear and grief. The innocence and openness of my son allowed him to experience the Comforter in his time of need. We, as adults, must also open ourselves to experience the invisible man inside of us as well.

11

I GET IT

PROVERBS 22:4-6

We had been going to church off and on since our oldest son was two years old. I knew that he knew the Word and understood parts of it. I also knew that by nature, he was always eager to learn. Even in school, he loved learning new things, which carried over into Bible study and Sunday school. However, his love of learning and the ability to comprehend almost anything was not evidence of personal experience with Jesus.

Our church is what some would consider nonconventional. There was an agenda, but we were good at allowing God's plan to supersede our program. Sunday after Sunday, God came in and moved in the service powerfully. I always wondered if my son was getting it or if he understood what was going on. When I would ask him, he would casually answer, "Yeah, I get it a little bit.

One evening, my 14-year-old son looked at me and said some of the most refreshing words I have ever heard him speak. He said, "Mom, service today was good. I get it." That day God gave a message through our dance ministry and even spoke through one of the members. As he proceeded to tell me that although he couldn't quite understand what God was saying, he knew that God was telling His people that they needed to do something, and there were no exceptions.

The Bible tells us to, "Start children off on the way they should go, and even when they are old they will not turn from it," Proverbs 22:6 NIV. It is only natural that parents question if they are doing the right things with their children. Am I praying enough, fellowshipping enough, or am I doing too much and pushing them away? There is no clear-cut answer. However, God always finds ways to confirm that what you are doing is pleasing in His sight. That conversation with my son that day proved to me that regardless of what mistakes he will make, he will always return to God because he gets it.

12
GROUND HOG DAY
LAMENTATION 3:20-23

I remember as a child that there was a movie called "Groundhog Day." The film was about a weatherman who was forced to live the same day over and over again. Initially, this was a very frustrating thing. However, he realizes that he is given several opportunities to get life right.

The plot of this movie makes me think of how merciful our God is. He gives us new mercies each day. This, of course, doesn't permit us to sin. Romans 6:1-2 lets us know that we shouldn't sin so that we can receive God's grace. Our ultimate goal is to strive to live each day as a representation of Christ. The reality is that we will make mistakes, miss opportunities to witness to someone, or get so caught up in our everyday lives that we forget to pray. Fortunately, despite what we do today, God loves us enough to let us start all over tomorrow.

PART III
FOLLOW

13

GPS (GOD'S POSITIONING SYSTEM)
PROVERBS 16: 1-9

I had to travel out of town for training. I was completely unfamiliar with the area, but praise God for modern technology. My GPS on my phone took me straight to my destination. I was obedient to the voice as it told me to turn left, turn right, take this exit, etc. I trusted that each step would get me to where I needed to be.

This made me think about my direction in life, and how trusting in God, I am. Proverbs 16:9 tells us that, "In their hearts humans plan their course, but the Lord establishes their steps." Most of us have an idea of where we would like to be in life, and ALL of us have a purpose. We must be willing to listen to God's voice as He gives us specific directions on how to get to His desired destination. Regardless of how unconventional the directions, we have to trust God to lead us exactly to where we need to be.

We trust technology to get us to our destination. How much more satisfying and fulfilling will it be to trust our God Positioning System to get us to our ultimate destination.

14

OIL CHANGE
1 CORINTHIANS 5:16-21

My husband and I were riding in the car one day when I asked why cars need oil changes and what the process was. He then explained to me that the oil runs through the engine and all the pistons while the vehicle is moving, which makes the oil dirty. The more a car is driven, the dirtier the oil gets, which may require it to get the oil changed more often for the car to continue to run correctly. When someone changes the oil, they empty all the old dirty oil and refill the engine with new clean oil.

As I listened to this explanation, it made me think about our lives in Christ and how we are renewed. In our initial acceptance of Christ, He cleansed us of all our sins. Just as 1 Corinthians

5:17 says, "Therefore, if anyone is in Christ, the new creation has come, the old has gone, the new is here!" However, being a believer doesn't exempt us from being run through the engine and pistons that life hands us. Daily, we are all at risk of dealing with stress, trauma, being mistreated, and physical ailments, just to name a few. These are things that can wear us out, drain us spiritually, or even cause us to feel unclean or unworthy. But Praise God, although being a believer, doesn't exempt us from the trials of life, it does offer us a chance to be refilled and to be renewed daily. Lamentations 3:22-23 states precisely that, "it is of the Lord's mercies that we are not consumed, because his compassions fail not. They are new every morning: great is thy faithfulness." God is more than willing and able to replenish us with precisely what we need to endure what life hands us every day. All we need to do is acknowledge that we need Him and ask Him to fill us with His clean oil. So when life is starting to beat you up, and you feel like you have nothing left to give, make sure you go to the Professional so that He can give you a spiritual oil change.

15
OPEN BOOK TEST
ROMANS 15:4-6

My sixth grader came home from school, telling me that he didn't do so well on an open book test. When I asked him why not, he replied, "Because I didn't feel like looking for all the answers." I immediately gave him an "are you serious," mom look. But just as God does in those moments, He gave me a glimpse of myself and my attitude toward life's challenges.

How often does life give us unexpected and challenging situations, and we immediately start to guess our way through it. All the tests that God gives us in life, He offers as an open book test. Romans 15:4 NIV states, "For everything that was written in the past was written to teach us, so that through endurance and the encouragement of the scriptures we might have hope." Just like my sixth-grader, we can develop the attitude of not feeling like looking up the answers in the Bible and try to figure things out on our own. God has given us His word to guide us through life. Because of how much God loves us, in addition to His Word, He gave us a guidance counselor in the Holy Spirit.

So, the next time life throws a pop quiz at you, remember to take advantage of the tools He has given you in the Bible and Holy Spirit. By following God's word and heeding to the Holy Spirit, you are guaranteed to pass.

16

UNREQUITED LOVE

JOHN 3: 16-18

I was scrolling through one of the social media sites reading people's comments. There was one young lady who wrote, "It hurts when he doesn't love you like you love him." I assumed that she was talking about some guy that she was in some sort of relationship with that did not feel as deeply for her as she did him.

At that moment, I felt a deep sorrow in my spirit. This wasn't a feeling of sorrow for this young lady whose heart may have been broken but for God. I thought about how horrible God must feel about His unrequited love. God gave His ONLY son to die for us(John 3:16). In return, all He wants us to do is to believe in Him and to love Him. As easy as it sounds, so many people do not know Him. What makes matters worse is the fact that believers are some of the biggest offenders. We live lives appearing to be so close to how the world is living, and we destroy the opportunity to be a witness to the people that don't know Jesus as their Savior. We even accept Jesus early in life, and as soon as a trial comes our way, we tuck tail and run, leaving God behind.

As life happens, we have to keep God in the forefront. We must remember how much HE loves us. We must visualize how Jesus suffered so that we don't have to just because of His love for us. Let us make sure that when God updates His relationship status with us, it says, "Deeply in love." The worst thing He could ever say is I never knew her/him.

17

BANKRUPTCY

ISAIAH 43: 15-19

*E*arly in our marriage, my husband and I made some very irresponsible decisions financially. We accumulated more debt than we had income. After years of poor choices and even worse money management, we were in over our heads. We had no choice but to file for Chapter 7 bankruptcy, which took all our debts and wiped them clean. We were given a fresh start in our credit, a chance to make it better. Through this process, my husband and I learned better ways to maintain our credit and live within our means.

God offers this world, in a sense, a chance to file Chapter 7 in life. John 3:16 says, "God so loved the world that He gave His only begotten son that whosoever believes in Him shall not perish but have everlasting life." God gave us Jesus to wipe the slate clean of all our sins. But wait, there's more, not only did He give His son to die in place of our sins. He offers us new mercies every day. God knows that we are only human, and we are guaranteed to mess up in some way every day. But praise God, because each day He wakes us up, is another chance to get it right. God allows us an unlimited amount of forgiveness once we have accepted Jesus as our Lord and Savior. Maybe you are perfect and don't make mistakes (which I doubt unless you are the Christ!). However, there are days where I am filing my bankruptcy paperwork several times an hour because I let life get the best of me, and I need to start over. So, I am grateful for God giving me an unlimited number of fresh starts that will last until He calls me home.

18

PRICELESS
PSALM 139: 13-16

I spend a lot of time with young teens and teenagers. I am the mother of a young teen and a teenager. I also help with a youth group at a local organization. I enjoy the time that I spend with them, along with the authentic and honest conversations that come with the time.

During one of our meetings, we were talking about self-worth. I asked the group, "If your boyfriend or girlfriend told you to give them your phone, would you? Would you let them have your phone and never return it?" These teens looked at me as if I had asked them to do the unthinkable. There was a unanimous, "No." Some even let me know how much their phone cost and that it was way too expensive too just give away. I then asked them, "If you had to put a price on yourself, then what would it be?" Everyone pretty much agreed that there wasn't a number large enough to buy them. I finally asked them, "So what you are saying is that you are worth more than your phone? You were able to put a monetary value on your phone. However, there isn't a number large enough for you. If this is the truth, then why would you give another person who does not value you all of you?" At that moment, I could see their minds working.

I reminded the group that they are like precious jewels to their Creator, and they were responsible for protecting that. They need to know that God took His time to "fearfully and wonderfully" make them. I hope that by recognizing God's love for them that they realize that they are truly priceless. They will no longer seek love from those who don't deserve them but find joy in the love of the Lord until the right one comes along. I want them to know that their worth is not determined by the number of people that say "I love you" but by being "the one whom Jesus loves. So, every now and then, I hear them whispering to each other the word "priceless" as a reminder of just how valuable they are.

ABOUT THE AUTHOR

Hello, my name is Shana Byrd. I was born and raised in Columbus, Ohio, and I am the youngest of 3. Growing up, my grandparents, who we lovingly referred to as Mommae and Daddy Ernest, lived the next street over and played a huge part in my upbringing. My brother, cousins, and I all stayed with our grandparents while our parents worked. It definitely made for some great childhood memories.

Although both of my parents were raised in the church, we didn't attend church regularly growing up. I credit Mommae and Daddy Ernest for introducing the concept of Jesus to me through conversation, gospel music, and of course, the occasional visit to Sunday service with them. I didn't know then, but those moments would be life-changing.

I became a mother at a young age, and the relationship with my son's father ended on rocky terms. That left me in a dark place and searching for something. In the midst of partying, I would attend random churches hoping to find some type of peace. I would spend the entire service crying and still leave full of sorrow. It wasn't until I went to Lord of Life Fellowship Church to impress a young man, who just so happened to be a PK (preacher's kid) that I found what I was looking for. I remember asking him what he told his dad about me because every time I visited, the message seemed to be directed towards me. After just a couple of months of visiting, I decided to give my life to Christ and join the church. My grandparents taught me the concept of Jesus, and it was the teachings that came from Lord of Life that helped me understand and develop a relationship with Jesus.

 Within a year after being saved, I married that young man! My husband Tim and I have now been married for 18 years. We have four amazing sons; Quoran 21, Timmy Shane 18, Makhi 15, and Nasir 14. As the ebbs and flows of life happen, it is the faces of these five men that continue to remind me of how awesome God truly is.

facebook.com/shana.bee.92

instagram.com/shanab94216

www.ingramcontent.com/pod-product-compliance
Lightning Source LLC
Chambersburg PA
CBHW052125110526
44592CB00013B/1761